SPECIAL LIVES IN HISTORY THAT BECOME

Signature LIVES

FREDERICK
DOUGLASS

SLAVE, WRITER, ABOLITIONIST

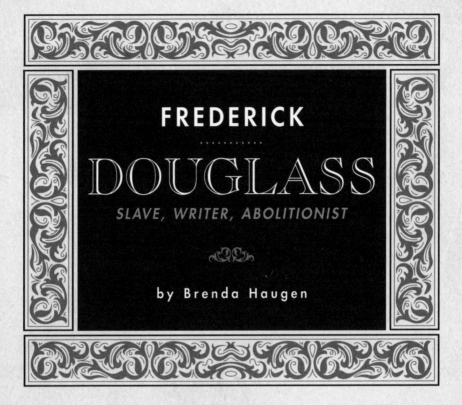

FREDERICK
DOUGLASS
SLAVE, WRITER, ABOLITIONIST

by Brenda Haugen

Content Adviser: Keith A. Mayes, Ph.D.,
Professor of African American & African Studies,
University of Minnesota

Reading Adviser: Rosemary G. Palmer, Ph.D.,
Department of Literacy, College of Education,
Boise State University

COMPASS POINT BOOKS ✦ MINNEAPOLIS, MINNESOTA

Compass Point Books
3109 West 50th Street, #115
Minneapolis, MN 55410

Visit Compass Point Books on the Internet at *www.compasspointbooks.com*
or e-mail your request to *custserv@compasspointbooks.com*

Editor: Sue VanderHook
Lead Designer: Jaime Martens
Photo Researcher: Marcie C. Spence
Page Production: Tom Openshaw, Bobbie Nuytten
Cartographer: XNR Productions, Inc.
Educational Consultant: Diane Smolinski

Managing Editor: Catherine Neitge
Art Director: Keith Griffin
Production Director: Keith McCormick
Creative Director: Terri Foley

To my cousin Tanya McCord, who has stood by me in good times and bad.
I love you! *BLH*

Library of Congress Cataloging-in-Publication Data
Haugen, Brenda
  Frederick Douglass / by Brenda Haugen.
    p. cm—(Signature lives)
  Includes bibliographical references and index.
  ISBN 0-7565-0818-5 (hardcover)
  1. Douglass, Frederick, 1818-1895—Juvenile literature. 2. African
American abolitioinists—Biography—Juvenile literature. 3. Abolitionists—
United States—Biography—Juvenile literature. 4. Antislavery move-
ments—United States—History—19th century—Juvenile literature. 5.
Slaves—Maryland—Biography—Juvenile literature. I. Title. II. Series.
  E449.D75H38 2005
  973.8'092—dc22   2004025341

CIVIL WAR ERA

The Civil War (1861-1865) split the United States into two countries and divided the people over the issue of slavery. The opposing sides—the Union in the North and the Confederacy in the South—battled each other for four long years in the deadliest American conflict ever fought. The bloody war sometimes pitted family members and friends against each other over the issues of slavery and states' rights. Some of the people who lived and served their country during the Civil War are among the nation's most beloved heroes.

Table of Contents

LIVING WITH CRUELTY 9

GROWING UP A SLAVE 15

LIFE AT THE GREAT HOUSE FARM 25

AN AWAKENING IN BALTIMORE 33

LIVING WITH A SLAVE BREAKER 43

FREEDOM 63

FREDERICK GETS A NEW NAME 71

FIGHTING FOR THE UNION CAUSE 85

LIFE AFTER THE WAR 91

LIFE AND TIMES 96

LIFE AT A GLANCE 102

ADDITIONAL RESOURCES 103

GLOSSARY 105

SOURCE NOTES 106

SELECT BIBLIOGRAPHY 108

INDEX 109

IMAGE CREDITS 112

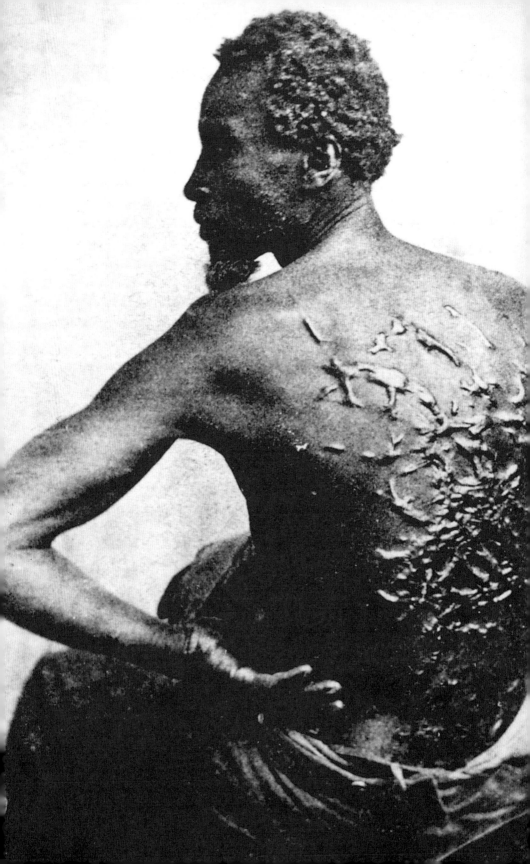

1 LIVING WITH CRUELTY

❧❦❧

Shaking and scared, the little boy hid in a closet. Despite the horror he had seen before slipping into his hiding place, Frederick Bailey tried to stay as quiet as he could. He heard the screams and curses, but he couldn't cry out loud or yell for the vicious man to stop. It wouldn't do any good. Frederick didn't want to be discovered and suffer the same punishment his Aunt Hester was enduring.

Captain Anthony let loose a string of curses as he continued to beat his slave. She cried for mercy, but Anthony possessed none. Hester's crime was leaving the plantation. Anthony was enraged because she had gone to see her boyfriend, another slave named Ned Roberts. Anthony specifically told

Marks of punishment on
the back of a slave

her she wasn't to see Roberts anymore. Because Anthony owned Hester, his word was law.

The beating started when Hester returned to the plantation. Anthony dragged her to a place in the kitchen designated for whipping slaves. He stripped Hester to her waist and made her stand on a stool. Forcing Hester to raise her arms, he tied her outstretched hands to a hook attached to a beam in the ceiling. With a long piece of leather, Anthony beat Hester's naked back until her blood covered the floor below.

Slaves gathered in front of plantation outbuildings in Beaufort, South Carolina.

Frederick couldn't get the sound of Hester's cries out of his head. He would always remember what he saw before taking refuge in the closet. This wouldn't be the last time he would experience the cruelty of slavery.

Facing a life of slavery since birth, Frederick could only dream of freedom. As a child, he wished for simple things—enough food to fill his hungry stomach and clothes to cover his body and keep him warm. He wanted to celebrate birthdays as white children did on the plantation. In fact, he didn't even know what day he was born. He knew he had been born in 1818 in Tuckahoe, Maryland, but no one was ever sure what day he came into the world. For slaves, birthdays ranked low in importance.

As he grew into a young man, Frederick's desire for freedom became stronger. His hopes were many—he wanted to be treated as a human being, and he wished he could keep the money he earned from his hard work. He yearned to be able to read. He longed to start a family of his own, one that couldn't be split up and sold at the whim of a cruel slave owner.

Frederick suffered beatings and humiliation at the hands of his owners. He sometimes tried to escape, patiently waiting for the right time to run away. At other times, he found ways to secretly educate himself. He quickly discovered that the ability to read and write was his key to freedom.

Although he wanted to leave his life of slavery, Frederick realized that running away meant leaving his friends behind and likely never seeing them again. While these thoughts filled his heart with sadness, Frederick decided that gaining his freedom was worth the pain. Later, he would realize that his freedom would allow him to help others in ways not possible when bound in the chains of slavery.

Frederick was caught in his first attempt to run away, but he was successful in another try. To avoid being found in the North, he changed his name to Frederick Douglass and lived as a fugitive. A U.S. law said slaves that were captured had to be returned to their owners.

Frederick Douglass as a young man

Though afraid someone would discover he was a runaway slave, Douglass decided he would not remain silent. Never again would he hide as he had that day in the closet when his aunt was beaten. He would speak out against slavery and publicly name those who treated him and his fellow slaves so horribly. What he revealed would help his listeners understand how cruel it was to enslave a whole group of people. Whenever he had a chance, he would strongly proclaim that this was a free country for all people.

Although risking his own safety, Douglass—runaway and fugitive slave—started an antislavery newspaper and gave speeches across the country. When the Civil War began, he enlisted a group of black men to fight for the Union cause. With great pride, Douglass welcomed one of his sons as the first black man to join the volunteer unit.

Douglass gave most of his life to the cause of freedom. He worked to liberate slaves from abuse like Aunt Hester had endured. He refused to leave anyone behind, no matter how much he had to sacrifice. ✑

2 Growing Up a Slave

❧⟨∾⟩❧

Slaves working in the heat of a cotton field in the southern United States was a common sight in the 1800s. Plantation owners like Edward Lloyd in Tuckahoe, Maryland, had slaves for every job. While some slaves toiled in the fields, others tended the gardens, worked in the carriage house and stables, and served in the kitchen.

Lloyd owned more than 1,000 slaves. Some worked on the home plantation; the rest lived and worked on Lloyd's smaller farms nearby. Twenty overseers were in charge, making sure, often with a whip, that slaves worked as hard as they could.

In February 1818, a slave named Harriet Bailey gave birth to a son on Lloyd's farm in Tuckahoe. All slaves were considered property, so this newborn merely added to Lloyd's wealth.

The birth of Frederick Augustus Washington Bailey wasn't officially recorded, so he would never be certain of his birthday. Slaves' birthdays weren't celebrated anyway. It wasn't a happy occasion when a slave was born into a life of misery.

Frederick was never sure who his father was. Anyone who ever spoke of his father said he was a white man. Rumor had it that his father was his master, but Frederick never knew which master and wasn't sure if the story was true.

Slaves often were separated from their families, and Frederick's experience was no different. Before he turned 1 year old, he was taken from his mother, who was sent to work on a farm 12 miles (19.3 km) from the main plantation. There she worked for Captain Aaron Anthony, hired by Lloyd to manage the farm.

Young slave children often were sent to live with the older slaves who were no longer able to work in the fields. Frederick's new home was a little shack on

From about 1500 to 1865, millions of Africans were captured and shipped to North and South America for slave labor. In the United States, nearly one in three people living in the South was a slave. Slavery continues to be used in some areas of the world today, including Sudan, Burma, and Pakistan. In Sudan, there is an Underground Railroad similar to what was used in the United States in the 1800s to help rescue slaves and take them to freedom.

the outskirts of the plantation near Tuckahoe Creek.
Frederick was fortunate, however, since the two old
slaves who lived there were his grandparents, Betsey
and Isaac Bailey.

Older slaves cared for the babies and young slave children on the plantation.

Sometimes Frederick's mother stole away in the
night to visit her little boy. Usually, she walked the
many miles that separated her from Frederick after
a long day in the fields. Harriet would curl up on the
floor with her young son until he drifted off to sleep.
Like other slaves, Frederick didn't have a bed. After
Frederick fell asleep, his mother would begin her

trek back to the farm. If she was not in the field by sunrise, she could count on a harsh whipping. Frederick didn't remember much about his mother, but later he did write:

> *I do not recollect of ever seeing my mother by the light of day. She was with me in the night. She would lie down with me, and get me to sleep, but long before I waked she was gone.*

Because he wasn't old enough to work, Frederick was rather carefree. He grew very close to his grandmother and enjoyed playing with the other children in her care. Like most of his friends, Frederick ran around barely clothed and sometimes even naked. Youngsters too small to work in the fields were given just two shirts a year. Slave owners didn't think children needed shoes, pants, socks, or jackets. Frederick didn't know about life outside the farm, so he didn't realize how poorly he was treated.

Frederick did know when he felt hungry or cold. On the Lloyd property, slaves were given a set amount of food. Each adult got 8 pounds (3.6 kg) of meat and one bushel of cornmeal to last the whole month. Clothes were passed out once a year. Each adult slave received one pair of light linen pants, one pair of winter pants, two linen shirts, one pair of socks, a pair of shoes, and a jacket. Each man and woman also got a blanket. The blankets were worse than the ones used to cover the horses, but slaves were glad to have anything. Children didn't get blankets. To keep warm, they had to use their imaginations. Later, Frederick remembered:

> *The children stuck themselves in holes and corners, about the quarters; often in the corner of the huge chimneys, with their feet in the ashes to keep them warm.*

When Frederick was only about 7 years old, his

A young slave keeps warm in a comfortless cabin.

mother died after suffering a long illness. Frederick was not allowed to visit her while she was sick and never said good-bye before she died. He wasn't allowed to go to her burial where she was placed in an unmarked grave. Since he only remembered seeing her a few times in his life, Frederick didn't feel much emotion when she died. He felt like she had been a stranger to him.

While he didn't grieve much over his mother's death, Frederick was overcome with sadness when he was separated from his grandmother. Frederick turned 8 years old, and Grandma Betsey was told to bring the young boy to the Great House Farm, the name for the Lloyd family plantation.

Plantations are large estates or farms where workers usually grow a single crop. Most plantations are located on fertile, flat land in warm regions of the world. Crops commonly grown on plantations are cotton, coffee, rice, sugar cane, and tropical fruits. Powerful landowners in the United States operated plantations with slave labor until slavery was abolished in 1865.

Although the trip to the Great House Farm was only 12 miles (19.3 km), it was a long journey for the little boy and his grandmother. Though a few gray hairs peeked out of the bandanna she wore on her head, Grandma Betsey was a strong woman. She carried Frederick on the journey whenever his little legs grew too tired to keep walking.

When the pair arrived at the Great House Farm, Frederick

This Maryland plantation in the 1800s had outbuildings and a main house.

was surprised by all the noise and activity. The plantation was like a big business with places for shoemaking, weaving, and grinding grain.

Frederick had never seen so many buildings. A large wooden structure called the main house stood majestically with its big columns and white paint. A well-kept lawn was interrupted by a variety of buildings, all of them clean and neat. Among the buildings were kitchens, washhouses, greenhouses, and a dairy. Pens enclosed an almost endless variety of birds, including turkeys, pigeons, and chickens.

The overseer lived in a big red house not far

from the huts where the slaves slept. Singing often erupted from the huts or from the fields where the slaves toiled. Slaves made up songs as they worked, telling in music about their joy and their sadness. All around, slaves bustled around doing their jobs, and children were everywhere. Frederick remembered:

In the 1870s, slaves lived in log cabins at the Hermitage, plantation home of U.S. President Andrew Jackson near Nashville, Tennessee.

> *I found myself in the midst of a group of children of many colors; black, brown, copper colored, and nearly white. I had not seen so many children before.*

A little overwhelmed by the new sights and

sounds, Frederick stuck close to Grandma Betsey. He was afraid she would be taken away from him if he dared to leave her side.

Still, his grandmother insisted Frederick go play. She pointed out his brother Perry and sisters Sarah and Eliza. Frederick heard he had a brother and sisters, but he didn't know what the words meant until now. Slaves who were separated from their mothers, fathers, brothers, and sisters, didn't understand what a family was. Frederick later wrote:

> *I had never seen my brother nor my sisters before; and, though I had sometimes heard of them, and felt a curious interest in them, I really did not understand what they were to me, or I to them.*

Frederick followed his grandmother's gentle order and went to play with the other children. Not long afterward, a child ran up to Frederick and told him his grandmother had left. Frederick couldn't believe it. After searching for her, he found it was true. Devastated, he fell to the ground and cried. ❧

3 LIFE AT THE GREAT HOUSE FARM

Frederick's home was now the Great House Farm. The workday started early there. Not a moment of daylight was wasted. At the crack of dawn, the overseer blew his horn. This signaled the slaves who worked in the fields to rush to their jobs. The overseer stood ready with a hickory stick and leather whip to beat anyone who was late, lagged behind, or overslept.

Slaves were usually hungry and cold, and they were also very tired. On the Lloyd plantation, more slaves were whipped for oversleeping than for any other offense. Slaves worked hard all day long, but their tasks didn't end when the sun went down. Well into the night, they did their own chores—cooking evening meals and mending clothes—

which left little time for sleep.

Slaves often ate breakfast and lunch wherever they happened to be working. In the fields, they might have a small piece of meat or fish, along with a type of bread called ash cakes. Just as its name implies, the bread was covered with ash from the way it was cooked. Frederick didn't have fond memories of it.

> *This bread ... would disgust and choke a northern man, but it is quite liked by the slave. They eat it with avidity [eagerness], and are more concerned about the quantity than about the quality.*

Frederick lived at the Great House Farm from the summer of 1824 to March 1826. Still too young to work in the fields, he was old enough to round up cows, clean, and run errands for Lucretia, Captain Anthony's daughter. Lucretia favored Frederick, often showing him kindness.

One of Frederick's jobs was chasing birds from the plantation's lush garden. Because the garden was so large and filled with produce, four men took care of it. Apples, oranges, asparagus, and other fruits and vegetables grew in abundance. The Lloyds's plentiful garden attracted visitors from miles around.

The Lloyd family had more food than they could use. Still, the garden was off-limits to the hungry

The Lloyd plantation today in Tuckahoe, Maryland.

slaves. If slaves were caught taking food from the garden, they could expect a severe beating. Lloyd even had the garden fence marked with tar. If a slave had tar on his clothes, Lloyd assumed he had been stealing from the garden and had him whipped.

Frederick's stomach almost always growled with hunger. Slave children ate from a trough out in the yard. With no forks or spoons to use, they grabbed whatever they could find to pick up the mush from the trough. Some used oyster shells or old shingles. Others used their hands.

"He that ate fastest got most; he that was strongest secured the best place; and few left the trough satisfied," Frederick wrote.

In his free time, Frederick went hunting with Lloyd's son Daniel. When Daniel shot a bird, Frederick ran to pick it up. Frederick didn't complain about this. After all, Daniel liked little Frederick and offered him a sweet treat once in a while. Daniel also kept other boys from picking on Frederick, and any protection a slave could get was welcome. Few slaves received such kindness.

In fact, they lived in constant fear of their masters. Just hearing the name Austin Gore struck fear in their hearts. This cruel, heartless man was an overseer on one of the outlying farms before coming to the Great House Farm.

A slave named Demby one day became the subject of Gore's wrath. To avoid a whipping, Demby ran into a nearby creek. Figuring Gore wouldn't come into the water after him, Demby refused to come out. Gore gave the slave until the count of three to get out or be shot. When Demby refused, Gore took aim and shot him dead. Frederick later gave the awful details about the incident:

Household slaves lived in loft areas over the plantation house kitchen, laundry room, or stable. They often worked seven days a week, although Sunday's tasks were somewhat less demanding. Slaves inside the house were usually female, while male slaves who didn't work in the fields served as coachmen or gardeners.

[I]n an instant poor Demby was no more. His mangled body sank out of sight, and blood and brains marked the water where he had stood.

Gore wouldn't be tried for murder for killing Demby because slaves weren't considered people. They were property. If a man killed another man's slave, he needed only to apologize or pay for the value of the slave. Such was the case with Demby, and it would be that way when Beal Bondly killed one of Lloyd's slaves.

Austin Gore prepares to shoot a slave named Demby.

Bondly's property bordered the Lloyd plantation. One of Lloyd's old slaves happened to go on the Bondly property one day to fish. Without any warning, Bondly shot and killed him. The next day, Frederick saw Bondly talking with Lloyd. Apparently they reached an agreement on the issue of compensation, because nothing was ever done about the incident.

Lloyd also treated the slaves with cruelty. He expected slaves to stand silent, listen, and tremble when he spoke. No one knew this rule better than Old Barney, the slave who tended the carriage house and stables on the Lloyd plantation.

The Lloyds owned three beautiful coaches and the best horses money could buy. Old Barney and his son Young Barney took special care of the animals. Yet Lloyd could always find something wrong with the horses if he felt like giving a beating. If a horse didn't look alert or well brushed, Lloyd would punish the slaves. They never knew what would upset their owner. Since they weren't allowed to defend themselves, slaves would helplessly listen and tremble as Lloyd made them suffer for their mistakes.

The master wouldn't stop with just hollering at the slaves. Frederick remembered a time when Lloyd forced Old Barney down to his knees and lashed the old slave on his naked shoulders for some imagined offense.

A busy port in Baltimore, Maryland, in the mid-1800s

Frederick was always afraid he would be the victim of such a beating, so he was thrilled when he heard he was being sent to Baltimore. There he would live with Hugh Auld, the brother of Thomas Auld, Lucretia's husband.

Frederick figured life in the Auld household couldn't be worse than it was at the Great House Farm. Besides, his mother had died, and he rarely got to see Grandma Betsey anymore. Leaving the plantation brought no feelings of sadness. In fact, Frederick looked forward to the adventure. 🐚

Chapter 4 An Awakening in Baltimore

Before leaving the Great House Farm, Frederick Bailey scrubbed his skin with a vigor he'd never had before. Lucretia said she'd give him his first pair of pants if he cleaned himself up for his trip to Baltimore. Frederick scrubbed harder, washing off the dirt, but also scraping off dead skin from his feet and knees. Sleeping on a cold, hard floor all his life had left his skin hard and crusty. "My feet have been so cracked with the frost, that the pen with which I am writing might be laid in the gashes," Frederick remembered.

It was 1826 when 8-year-old Frederick boarded Lloyd's ship, the *Sally Lloyd*, and sailed to Baltimore. The ship usually carried corn, wheat, and tobacco to market, but on this day, the *Sally Lloyd*

Frederick learned to read from his master's wife, Sophia Auld, in Baltimore.

On the Chesapeake
Bay, Baltimore became
an important harbor
community in the
American colonies.
Soon after the city was
founded in 1729,
Baltimore developed a
major shipbuilding
industry. The city
became famous in the
early 1800s for the clip-
per ships built there.

was delivering sheep to the slaughterhouse—and Frederick to his new master.

After helping take the animals to the slaughterhouse, Frederick arrived at his new home on Alliciana Street. Unsure what to expect, his fear disappeared when Mr. and Mrs. Hugh Auld answered the door. Their son, little Thomas Auld, was there, too. Frederick would be expected to help raise him. Hugh Auld appeared to be kind, and his wife Sophia looked like an angel. Frederick was overjoyed with his good luck. "I was utterly astonished at her goodness," Frederick wrote. "I scarcely knew how to behave towards her."

Never having owned a slave before, Sophia Auld wasn't sure how to treat Frederick. She didn't like how he avoided her eyes, and she felt uncomfortable when he trembled and spoke to her with fear in his voice. Years of abuse had trained Frederick to talk and act this way toward whites. But Sophia expected him to look her in the eyes and not be afraid to speak. Frederick found this shocking, but he liked it very much.

Sophia was sad that Frederick didn't know how

to read. She believed he should at least be able to read the Bible. On the plantation, reading was a privilege reserved for the white folks. Some slaves, like Frederick's mother, had found secret ways to learn how to read and write. Unfortunately, she never got a chance to teach her son those skills.

In his new home in Baltimore, Frederick liked to listen to Sophia read the Bible aloud. Hearing her read awakened a desire in him to read, too. When he got enough courage, he asked Sophia to teach him to read. She readily agreed.

Frederick Douglass's Bible is inscribed: "Presented to the Hon. Frederick Douglass by Members of the Metropolitan A.M.E. Church, Washington DC."

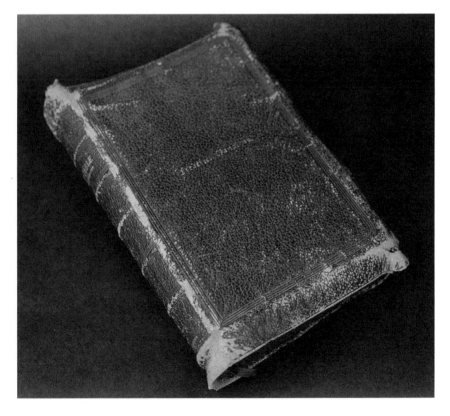

At first, Frederick learned the alphabet. With Sophia's help and encouragement, he soon began reading small words. Frederick remembered how pleased Sophia was with his progress:

> *My mistress seemed almost as proud of
> my progress, as if I had been her own
> child, and supposing that her husband
> would be as well pleased, she made no
> secret of what she was doing for me.*

When Auld found out his wife was educating
Frederick, he was very upset. Teaching slaves
led to trouble, Auld said. Once slaves learned to
read, Auld believed, they would never be satisfied with their lives anymore. He thought they
would become unmanageable and worthless.
Sophia was surprised by her husband's outburst,
but she respected what he said. She quit teaching Frederick.

Frederick was listening with surprise to
everything Auld said. But he knew that what
Auld said was true. An educated man would
never be happy bound by the chains of slavery.
That was why plantation owners refused to let
slaves learn to read and write. Auld's tirade
made Frederick determined to educate himself.
That would be his way out of slavery.

Since Sophia could no longer teach him to
read, Frederick came up with a plan. He made
friends with white children and asked them to
teach him how to read. When children didn't want
to help him, he bribed them with the good bread
from the Auld household. The poor white chil-

dren in Baltimore were always glad to get some extra bread.

Since Auld's outburst, Sophia had kept Frederick from reading anything around the house. So Frederick secretly carried a book with him when he ran errands. He would finish his tasks as quickly as possible and use the rest of the time to read.

Owning a slave changed Sophia. She no longer remained as sweet and good-hearted as she was when Frederick arrived. The change saddened the young slave, but Frederick was changing, too. He read about emancipation in a book called *The Columbian Orator* and began to believe that he might not have to remain a slave his entire life. Reading opened his eyes to how unfair it was to be in bondage. He grew to hate slaveholders.

> *I could regard them in no other light than a band of successful robbers, who had left their homes, and gone to Africa, and stolen us from our homes, and in a strange land reduced us to slavery. I loathed them as being the meanest as well as the most wicked of men.*

Yet even with the knowledge he gained, Frederick still did not know how to change his lowly condition. He soon received the encouragement he needed, however. He heard about aboli-

An etching of young sailors at a wharf in Baltimore, Maryland

tionists—people who believed that slavery was shameful and should be eliminated.

Among the abolitionists he met was a pair of Irishmen unloading a boat on Baltimore's wharf. Frederick enjoyed spending time around the ships, and when he saw the men working, he trotted over to help. While talking to the Irishmen, Frederick mentioned that he was a slave. With disgust, they

Harriet Tubman (1820?-1913) was born a slave in Bucktown, Maryland. Escaping from slavery in 1849, she returned to help hundreds of slaves run away from their owners and go to free states or Canada. Tubman never was caught and never lost a slave on any of her 19 freedom trips. She became the most famous leader of this secret escape system known as the Underground Railroad. Blacks called her Moses, after the biblical figure who led the Israelites out of bondage in Egypt.

told him that such a fine young man should not live his life without freedom.

Frederick was surprised when they suggested that he try to escape to the North. He didn't know what the North was, and he didn't know that Maryland wasn't considered a Northern state. Once there, the men said, Frederick could find help through the Underground Railroad. As Frederick would discover, the Underground Railroad was not underground, nor was it a railroad. It was a secret way for slaves to escape to the Northern states and Canada, where they could be free.

Frederick listened closely to what the men said, but he didn't show his excitement. He'd heard plenty of stories about tricky white men who encouraged slaves to escape and even helped them make plans to run away. Then, when the slave made a dash for freedom, the white men quickly captured the slave and collected a hefty reward from the grateful master. Though Frederick

A painting by Charles Webber titled "The Underground Railroad" shows black slaves escaping to the North in harsh winter weather.

wanted to trust these Irishmen, he decided to be safe and keep his mouth shut. He later wrote:

> *I was afraid that these seemingly good men might use me so; but I nevertheless remembered their advice, and from that time I resolved to run away.*

Frederick made sure the Aulds didn't find out what he had learned at the wharf that day. But he would never forget it. ℘

5 LIVING WITH A SLAVE BREAKER

College

~~~~~~

After living with the Aulds in Baltimore for about three and a half years, Frederick found himself back at the Great House Farm. Captain Anthony had died, and his property was going to be divided between his two surviving children, Lucretia and Andrew. Frederick was still considered Anthony's property, so he had to return to the plantation to be formally counted along with Anthony's other possessions.

The idea of returning to the Great House Farm caused great fear in Frederick's heart. He remembered the kindness Lucretia had shown him, but he also remembered her brother Andrew, an evil, drunken man. Not long after Frederick returned to the plantation, Andrew made an example of Frederick's brother Perry. Andrew grabbed the boy by the throat, threw him to the ground, and stomped on his head with the heel of his boot. As blood ran from the child's ears and nose, Andrew glared at a horrified Frederick and told him he'd suffer the same fate.

The day finally came for a price to be determined for the plantation. Anthony's property was grouped together according to value. Slaves were mixed with pigs, cattle, and other items. As the property was divided, Frederick prayed with all his heart that he would fall into Lucretia's hands and not Andrew's. His prayers were more than answered. Not only did Frederick go to Lucretia, she sent him right back to the Aulds in Baltimore.

However, Frederick's good fortune didn't last long. Shortly after he returned to Baltimore, Lucretia died, leaving her husband Thomas Auld as Frederick's owner. Auld soon remarried and went to live with his new wife, Rowena Hamilton Auld, on a plantation in St. Michaels, Maryland. In March 1833, 15-year-old Frederick traveled to St. Michaels to live with his new owner.

Frederick found the Aulds to be evil people. Thomas Auld was quick to use the whip when he wasn't satisfied with Federick's work. Frederick regretted he had not tried to run away while he was still in Baltimore. It would have been easier to escape in a bustling city than in the open country.

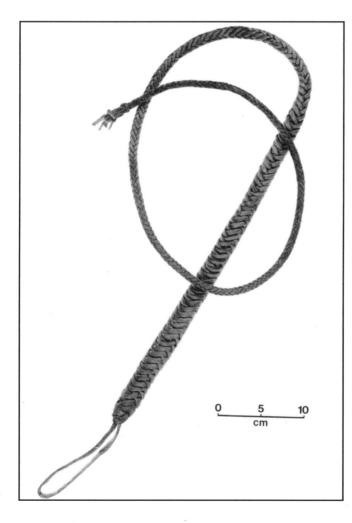

Slaves didn't get enough to eat at the Auld plantation. The food was usually rotten by the time it was delivered to the slaves. Frederick often was forced to beg or steal from other slaves to get enough food to stay alive.

After owning Frederick for nine months, Auld was still unsatisfied with his work. So he sent him to

The whip used by an overseer to punish slaves was made of hard braided ox hide. The 3-foot (91.4-cm) whip narrowed to the tip, where small strips of leather stuck out. This caused the victim of a whipping a great deal of pain.

a slave breaker. A slave breaker's job was to crush a slave's spirit and make him manageable. At first, Frederick was happy about the change:

> *I nevertheless made the change gladly, for I was sure of getting enough to eat, which is not the smallest consideration to a hungry man.*

Frederick, who was just 16 years old, reported on January 1, 1834, to Edward Covey's farm near the Chesapeake Bay in Maryland. His only possessions were a few pieces of clothes he carried on the end of a stick. Looking like a hobo, he walked to his new home 7 miles (11.3 km) away.

Covey, a poor farmer who rented the farmland as well as the slaves who worked it, was well-known for his ability to break young slaves. Here, Frederick became a field slave for the first time. His one-year stay at Covey's proved to be a nightmare. At daybreak on the first day, Covey sent Frederick into the forest to fill a cart with wood. Two untrained oxen were attached to the cart. Frederick had never worked with oxen, and these large animals had never

Andrew Jackson (1767-1845), president of the United States from 1829-1837, was a slave owner. His plantation was located near Nashville, Tennessee. In his will, Jackson left several slaves to his grandchildren and daughter-in-law.

worked with people. His mission was doomed before it even started.

Covey told Frederick that no matter what the oxen did, he shouldn't let go of the rope that held them. With this in mind, Frederick set off for the woods more than a mile away. The bitter cold cut through his thin clothing, but that was the least of his worries.

At first, all went amazingly well. Keeping the oxen in check, Frederick made it to the forest with-

In the 1860s, slaves used oxen-drawn carts to attempt to escape to free states.

Slaves forced to work on plantations were often whipped by cruel overseers.

out incident. But when the oxen were startled by something, Frederick didn't have time to think. The strong animals bolted as he tried desperately to hold on to the rope. The oxen raced into the forest, the cart smashing against trees and bouncing over stumps. Frederick believed he was about to die. He knew how easily he could be trampled under the hooves of the animals, crushed by the cart, or smacked into a tree.

The wild ride ended when the oxen became tangled in a dense group of trees. By now, the damaged cart had overturned. Frederick righted the cart and untangled the wild oxen. With that accomplished, he loaded the cart with as much wood as it could carry, hoping the weight of the cart would make the crazy animals settle down.

Frederick soon discovered how wrong he was. He got the oxen and cart out of the forest and to the gate, but the animals took off again, nearly crushing him against the gate.

When Frederick finally got back to the Covey house, he explained what happened, but Covey ordered him to take the oxen and cart back to the woods. This time, Covey came, too. Frederick remembered the incident well.

> *Just as I got into the woods, he came up and told me to stop my cart, and that he would teach me how to trifle away my time, and break gates. He then went to a large gum-tree, and with his axe cut three large switches, and, after trimming them up neatly with his pocket-knife, he ordered me to take off my clothes. I made him no answer, but stood with my clothes*

on. He repeated his order. I still made him no answer, nor did I move to strip myself. Upon this he rushed at me with the fierceness of a tiger, tore off my clothes, and lashed me till he had worn out his switches, cutting me so savagely as to leave the marks visible for a long time after.

Covey wasn't a big man, but he was frightening. His small greenish-gray eyes and his voice that sounded like a dog's growl made his slaves nervous. Covey would crawl on his belly through the fields, watching and surprising the slaves as they worked. He delighted in catching them slowing down. The slaves aptly nicknamed him "the snake."

Frederick's first day proved how miserable life with Covey would be. While the slaves at Covey's farm rose for work before sunrise, they often toiled until midnight. They didn't dare take a break. Getting a full five minutes in the field for lunch or dinner was a luxury. Frederick recalled later:

Mr. Covey succeeded in breaking me. I was broken in body, soul and spirit. I was completely wrecked, changed and bewildered; goaded almost to madness at one time, and at another reconciling myself to my wretched condition.

The one bright spot at Covey's was the farm's

An overseer whips a slave for returning late from seeing his wife.

location near the Chesapeake Bay. Frederick could see the beautiful sailing ships out on the water. With tears in his eyes, he dreamed of the freedom the boats represented and promised himself he wouldn't die a slave.

As time went on, things got worse for Frederick. Working outside on a particularly hot day, he became sick. When Covey discovered

Frederick had quit working, he kicked him in the side. Frederick tried to get up, but his strength left him. He fell back to the ground where he suffered another kick. After managing to get up on his feet, Frederick soon staggered and fell again. Picking up a board, Covey brutally struck him on the head. As blood flowed from his head wound, Frederick made no more attempts to stand up. Covey left him there to bleed.

Afraid he would die, the beaten slave decided his only chance of survival was to get up and walk 7 miles (11.3 km) to St. Michaels. He hoped his master Thomas Auld would take pity on him.

After staggering along the road for five hours, Frederick finally got to the Auld house. He begged Auld to send him anywhere but Covey's, where he feared he would be killed. Frederick described his condition.

> *From the crown of my head to my feet, I was covered with blood. My hair was all clotted with dust and blood; my shirt was stiff with blood. I suppose I looked like a man who had escaped a den of wild beasts, and barely escaped them.*

Despite Frederick's appearance, Auld thought he was exaggerating. If Frederick didn't shape up and follow Covey's rules, Auld said he would beat

Frederick himself. The shocked slave couldn't believe what he was hearing. He had nowhere to turn. He'd have to go back to Covey in the morning.

When Frederick arrived back at the farm, Covey ran after him with a whip. Frederick hid in a nearby cornfield until the slave breaker got tired of looking for him. Taking his chances on starvation rather than going back to certain death, Frederick headed into the woods.

A slave hides in the field as he is pursued by his captors.

> *"Memory was given to man for some wise purpose. The past is the mirror in which we may discern the dim outlines of the future."*
>
> **Frederick Douglass**

In the dark, Frederick happened upon another slave, Sandy Jenkins. He was walking through the woods on his way to visit his wife, a free woman who lived about 4 miles (6.5 km) away. Jenkins invited Frederick to come with him, and Frederick gladly accepted the invitation.

After eating and getting cleaned up a bit, Frederick told Jenkins about his situation. Jenkins persuaded Frederick to go back to Covey, since he really had no other choice. On Sunday morning, Frederick took Jenkins's advice and headed back to the slave breaker's farm. Covey ignored him the whole day.

The situation changed on Monday, however. As Frederick tended to a horse, Covey attacked him. At that moment, Frederick resolved to fight back. Seizing Covey by the throat, Frederick rose with great strength and determination. The battle lasted nearly two hours, but Covey finally gave up. He never touched Frederick again.

The fight with Covey became the turning point in Frederick's life, and the fires of freedom burned in his soul. His sense of manhood was revived. Self confident and determined to be free, Frederick promised himself he would never be beaten again.

> *I felt as I never felt before. It was a glorious resurrection, from the tomb of slavery, to the heaven of freedom. My long-crushed spirit rose, cowardice departed, bold defiance took its place; and I now resolved that, however long I might remain a slave in form, the day had passed forever when I could be a slave in fact.*

Six months after the fight, Frederick's time with Covey finally drew to an end. Frederick returned to Thomas Auld, who hired him out to William Freeland, the owner of a farm about 3 miles (4.8 km) from St. Michaels. Frederick wrote:

> *My treatment, while in his employment was heavenly, compared with what I experienced at the hands of Mr. Edward Covey. I will give Mr. Freeland the credit of being the best master I ever had, till I became my own master.*

At Freeland's farm, the slaves were close like a family. Frederick now worked with his friend Sandy Jenkins, the slave he had met in the woods. Other friends included Henry Harris, John Harris, Charles Roberts, and Henry Bailey.

After a year at Freeland's farm, Frederick grew anxious to run away. Although Freeland treated the slaves well, they still longed to be free. While they dreaded the thought of getting caught, some of the slaves decided they would run away.

Young slaves attempt to escape to the North through the Southern swamps.

Using his writing skills, Frederick created passes for each of them. Slaves carried passes

given to them by their masters to prove to any white person that they had permission to travel. On the fake passes, Frederick wrote that the men could travel to Baltimore for Easter. In reality, they planned to find a way to Europe, since they didn't know about the Underground Railroad and freedom in the North and Canada.

The day before Easter drew near, and the slaves were excited and scared. Frederick wrote:

> On their journey to freedom on the Underground Railroad, runaway slaves found protection at safe houses. A lantern on the hitching post identified a safe house. Although harboring fugitive slaves was a crime, owners of safe houses thought slavery was wrong and believed they were doing the right thing.

Friday night was a sleepless one for me. I probably felt more anxious than the rest, because I was, by common consent, at the head of the whole affair. The responsibility of success or failure lay heavily on me.

Early Saturday morning, Frederick headed to a field, just as he always did. The horn sounded, and the slaves went to the house for breakfast. When he reached the house, Frederick was struck with fear. Freeland and another slave owner named Hamilton were walking from the barn toward the house. Three policemen followed. The slave owners had suspected the slaves were plotting an escape, and they thought Frederick was the ringleader.

Before the slaves could react, the policemen tied Frederick's wrists and bound John Harris. But Henry Harris refused to be tied up without a fight. Even after the two officers drew their guns and threatened to shoot him, Henry stood his ground. "Shoot me!" he yelled at them. "You can't kill me but once."

Henry knocked the pistols from the policemen's hands. In the scuffle that followed, Frederick managed to throw his fake pass into the

Slave owners advertised large rewards for the capture of their escaped slaves.

$200 REWARD!

RANAWAY from the subscriber, living near Upper Marlboro', Prince George's County, Md., on the 22d of Sept., 1861, my negro man **JOHN**, who calls himself *JOHN LEE*. He is 24 years old, a little below the ordinary height, well built; has a remarkable fine set of teeth, which he shows when talking, and of very smiling countenance. Said negro was hired at the time he left to Mr. John A. Frasier, in Surratts District. Also, my negro man **ANDREW**, who calls himself *ANDREW AMBUSH*. He ranaway on the 1st of January, 1862. He is about 23 years old, tall and slender built, quite black, long thick lips, full suit of hair

I will give the above reward for the apprehension of said negroes, or $100 for either of them, provided they are delivered to me or secured in jail, so that I get them again.

              WILLIAM P. PUMPHREY.

Welwood, Jan. 22, 1862.

fireplace. The passes were the only evidence the police needed to show the slaves truly had planned an escape.

After subduing Henry Harris, the policemen pushed the slaves to the door. William Freeland's mother Betsy yelled at Frederick for getting Henry and John into trouble. She shouted angrily:

> *You devil! You yellow devil! It was you that put it into the heads of Henry and John to run away. ... Henry nor John would never have thought of such a thing.*

As she cursed Frederick, she slipped some biscuits to Henry and John, who hadn't had their breakfast. Feeling powerless, Frederick secretly whispered to the two slaves to stick their fake passes in the biscuits and eat them. This would destroy proof of their plans, and perhaps they wouldn't be punished. Henry and John did what Frederick said. Their passes weren't discovered, but all three men still were punished. They were tied to two other slaves, Charles Roberts and Henry Bailey, who already had been arrested for their part in the escape plot. As the five barefooted slaves were dragged brutally down the road, people shouted insults at them. Apparently, everyone knew about their plan to run away. Some yelled that Frederick should be hanged—or worse.

This slave was up for sale, but first the slave trader examined him to make sure he was in good health.

"We were to be dragged that morning fifteen miles behind horses, and then to be placed in the Easton jail," Frederick remembered.

About 20 minutes after Frederick and his friends arrived at the jail, slave traders lined up to

get a look at them. Traders always watched for possible slaves to buy. Before they could be sold, though, Freeland and Hamilton took four of their slaves home. Frederick, however, remained in jail. He wrote about this discouraging time alone in the cell:

> *I was now left to my fate. I was all alone, and within the walls of a stone prison.... I thought the possibility of freedom was gone.*

Frederick endured jail for about a week when, to Frederick's surprise, Thomas Auld came to get him. He planned to sell Frederick back to his brother Hugh Auld in Baltimore. Thomas Auld was afraid he might lose his slave to angry community members set on killing Frederick. Baltimore would be a safer place. Frederick couldn't believe his good fortune. ✍

6 FREEDOM

ⰽⲋⲭⳑ

Frederick Bailey was glad to go back to the Hugh Auld home in Baltimore. Since the family didn't need him to watch their son Thomas any longer, Frederick had to look for a job. He would work outside the Auld home but turn his pay over to his owner at the end of the week.

It didn't take long for Frederick to find work. Baltimore's shipyard bustled with activity, and another set of hands was almost always welcome. Shipbuilder William Gardner hired Frederick, but first Frederick would have to work as an apprentice. For eight months, he learned about ships from the other men on Gardner's crew. Frederick completed whatever tasks needed to be done, although sometimes he found the work more than he could handle.

Frederick Douglass in 1855, at the
age of 37

My situation was a most trying one. At times I needed a dozen pairs of hands. I was called a dozen ways in the space of a single minute.

Frederick also struggled with his work for other reasons—white apprentices didn't want to work next to a black man. They vowed to make life miserable for him, but Frederick stuck to his promise that he would

Frederick Douglass worked as an apprentice at the shipyards in Baltimore, Maryland, where ships similar to this 19th-century whaler were docked.

never take a beating again without putting up a fight.

When four white apprentices threatened Frederick with bricks, sticks, and other weapons, he tried to protect himself. But he stood no chance in a four-against-one battle. After being struck on the head with one of their weapons, Frederick dropped to the ground. The apprentices fell upon him, pounding him with their fists. Frederick tried to rise, but one of the men kicked him in the eye. Later, he remembered his condition.

> *My eyeball seemed to have burst. When they saw my eye closed, and badly swollen, they left me. With this I seized the handspike, and for a time pursued them. But here the carpenters interfered, and I thought I might as well give it up.*

The beating was witnessed by dozens of white men, but no one came to Frederick's aid. In fact, some of them shouted that Frederick should be killed because he had raised his hand against a white man.

Afraid there might be more violence, Frederick found a way to get to the Aulds. He would always remember the kindness Sophia showed him that day.

> *The heart of my once overkind mistress was again melted into pity. My puffed-out eye and blood-covered face moved her to tears. She took a chair by me, washed the*

*blood from my face, and, with a mother's
tenderness, bound up my head, covering the
wounded eye with a lean piece of fresh beef.*

Hugh Auld decided Frederick wouldn't work for
Gardner again. After he recovered from his wounds,
Frederick got a job working for Walter Price, who
taught Frederick to caulk ships, making them watertight vessels.

As time passed, Frederick again longed for freedom. He hated giving his earnings to Auld at the end
of the week. He hated being told where he could go
and when to be home. As anger burned in his heart,
he determined to make a break for freedom. He
chose a date—September 3, 1838—as the day he
would run.

He look forward to September 3, but thinking
about it also made him sad. Despite his strong desire
to escape slavery, Frederick realized he would have
to leave the friends he had made in Baltimore. He
had also fallen in love with Anna Murray, a free
black woman he had met there. If his escape plan
failed, he might never see his friends or Anna again.
Yet if he didn't try, he could never hope for a happy
life with Anna and the family he'd always dreamed
about having someday.

Frederick's mind was made up. On September 3,
he borrowed papers from a free black sailor friend.
Dressed as a sailor and talking like one, too,

A newspaper cartoon shows how black people were forced off railroad cars.

Frederick drew no suspicion as he boarded a train bound for New York City. When the train conductor asked for his ticket and proof he could travel, Frederick handed over the borrowed papers. After a quick glance at the document, the conductor moved on to the next passenger. Finally, Frederick arrived in New York City.

Frederick Douglass lived as a slave in Maryland and as a fugitive in New York City and New Bedford, Massachusetts.

In less than a week after leaving Baltimore, I was walking amid the hurrying throng, and gazing upon the dazzling wonders of Broadway.

Frederick felt safe in New York, but he was still afraid. A 1793 law required that fugitive slaves who

were captured had to be returned to their owners. Though Frederick had escaped and now went by the name Frederick Johnson, he wasn't free in the eyes of the law. He went from being a slave to a fugitive, still living in fear.

> *I was afraid to speak to any one for fear of speaking to the wrong one, and thereby falling into the hands of money-loving kidnappers, whose business it was to lie in wait for the panting fugitive, as the ferocious beasts of the forest lie in wait for their prey.*

Frederick found safe haven with David Ruggles, a member of the Underground Railroad. Sympathetic with the plight of fugitive slaves, Ruggles gladly gave Frederick a safe place to stay. After learning that Frederick had experience with ships, Ruggles suggested he go to New Bedford, Massachusetts, where he'd easily find a job.

Frederick agreed, but he had something very important to do before he left New York. He wrote to Anna Murray and asked her to join him. She reached New York as quickly as she could, and on September 15, 1838, they were married. ✍

Frederick Douglass

Chapter

7 FREDERICK GETS A NEW NAME

❧❧❧

With a marriage certificate and $5 from Ruggles, the newlyweds boarded a steamboat on the first leg of their journey to New Bedford, Massachusetts. There, they would start their new life together.

In New Bedford, the couple went by the names Frederick and Anna Johnson. They soon discovered, however, that many people had the surname Johnson. Even Mary and Nathan Johnson, the generous couple who was giving them a place to live, had that name.

Frederick decided that in return for his kindness, Nathan Johnson should decide on his new surname. Nathan immediately chose Douglass, the name of a character in the book he was reading. The name fit—Frederick Douglass.

The Douglasses were happy with their new name. They also were happy with the beautiful community of New Bedford with its cozy homes and lovely churches. Douglass would visit the seashore and gaze at large, beautiful ships bobbing on the water. He later remembered how the people there lived:

Anna Murray Douglass, wife of Frederick Douglass

Every thing looked clean, new and beautiful. I saw few or no dilapidated houses, with poverty-stricken inmates; no half-naked children and barefooted women, such as I had been accustomed to see in Hillsborough, Easton, St. Michael's, and Baltimore. The people looked more able, stronger, healthier, and happier, than those of Maryland. I was for once made glad by a view of extreme wealth, without being saddened by seeing extreme poverty.

Many fugitive slaves found refuge in New Bedford and made wonderful lives for themselves. As Ruggles predicted, Douglass found a job right away. He got a job on a ship that carried oil. He could not have been happier. Douglass marveled:

> *It was new, dirty, and hard work for me; but I went at it with a glad heart and a willing hand. I was now my own master.... I worked that day with a pleasure I had never before experienced. I was at work for myself and newly-married wife. It was to me the starting-point of a new existence.*

Douglass now was earning money and keeping it. Soon, one more dream would become a reality— his dream of having a family. A daughter, Rosetta, was born in 1839. The following year, the young couple was blessed with a second child—Lewis.

Although happy with his job and growing family, Douglass could not forget the slaves still in bondage. Soon, Douglass discovered a group that shared his concern—the abolitionist movement. He read about the movement in William Lloyd Garrison's weekly newspaper, *The Liberator*. After hearing Garrison speak, Douglass wanted to help this famous abolitionist and do whatever he could to put an end to slavery.

Now that he had tasted the life of a free man, Frederick Douglass wanted other slaves to be able to break their chains of servitude. In the summer of 1841, a convention of the Massachusetts Anti-Slavery Society was held on Nantucket Island,

Massachusetts. William Lloyd Garrison would be there, along with abolitionist William C. Coffin and others who supported freedom for slaves.

Leaving Anna home with their two children, 23-year-old Douglass eagerly left for the meeting. He intended to listen to the speakers and learn about the antislavery movement. Douglass was taken by surprise, however, when Coffin asked him to speak. Coffin had heard Douglass speak to several black friends at a New Bedford meeting, and he knew Douglass's life story would inspire those at the Nantucket gathering. Nothing was more powerful to the cause of abolition than stories told by people who had escaped from slavery.

At first, Douglass hesitated. He had never spoken to a large gathering, particularly where white people were present. Parts of his story couldn't be shared since he was a fugitive, and information about where he came from and who his owner was would put him in danger. He could be captured and sent back to Maryland. If slaveholders knew how he had escaped, they might stop others from doing the same thing.

Despite his fears, Douglass got up to speak and captivated the audience with his story. Even without sharing all the details, Douglass's story was powerful. One of the members of the society, John A. Collins, approached Douglass with a job opportunity. How would he like to get paid to travel around the country telling his story? Douglass doubted he could do much good but agreed to try. He figured he'd quickly wear out his usefulness. After telling his story for a few months, people would tire of him. But he couldn't have been more wrong. He ended up speaking for the rights of black people for the rest of his life.

In the fall of 1841, the Douglasses moved to

Frederick Douglass spoke publicly about his experiences as a slave.

Lynn, Massachusetts. There, they lived in a nice home that friends in the antislavery movement helped them find. Over the next three years, two more children were added to the Douglass family. Joining Rosetta and Lewis were Frederick Jr. and Charles. Douglass's family was growing, and his life was changing. As he learned and grew as a person, Douglass wanted to do more than just tell his story. He realized the impact his words had on people, and he wanted to share more of his thoughts and ideas. His abolitionist friends warned him not to sound too smart and to stick to his life story. If he sounded too educated, they said, people wouldn't believe him. Douglass later realized they were right:

The *Anti-Slavery* Society, founded in Philadelphia in 1833 and led by William Lloyd Garrison, vowed to end slavery in the United States. Members of the society argued that slavery was illegal if it was not allowed in the Constitution. By 1838, the society had more than 250,000 members.

At last the apprehended trouble came. People doubted if I had ever been a slave. They said I did not talk like a slave, look like a slave, nor act like a slave.

After lecturing in the Northern states for nearly four years, Douglass decided he would no longer be afraid to tell the secret details of his life as a slave. In a historic speech in New York City, he shared specific

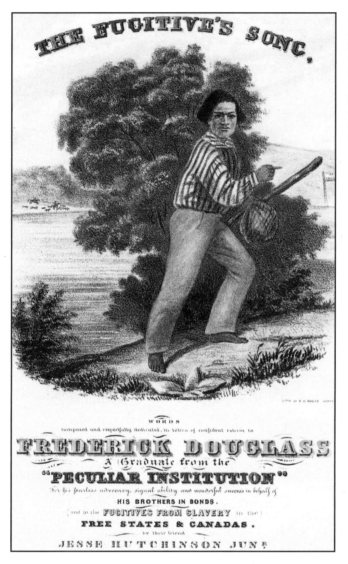

Frederick Douglass was pictured on the cover of an abolitionist song sheet published in Boston, Massachusetts in 1845.

information about his past that could lead to his arrest. He was surrounded most of the time by friends who would fight for his freedom, but Douglass still lived in fear that news of his whereabouts would reach his owner.

By 1845, Douglass had written and published his life story, *Narrative of the Life of Frederick Douglass, an American Slave*. In it he revealed the details of his life as a slave under cruel masters. The book flew off store shelves. In the first four months, about 5,000 copies were sold in the United States and Europe.

Now that it was well known that Douglass was a fugitive slave, his abolitionist friends feared for his safety. In August 1845, they sent him on a speaking tour of Great Britain, a place where slavery had been

The title page of Frederick Douglass's first autobiography, Narrative of the Life of Frederick Douglass, an American Slave

NARRATIVE

OF THE

LIFE

OF

FREDERICK DOUGLASS,

AN

AMERICAN SLAVE.

WRITTEN BY HIMSELF.

BOSTON:
PUBLISHED AT THE ANTI-SLAVERY OFFICE.
No. 25 CORNHILL
1845.

outlawed for 38 years. Douglass enjoyed enormous popularity in England. People lined up to hear him speak. He later recalled:

> *Great surprise was expressed by American newspapers, north and south, during my stay in Great Britain, that a person so illiterate and insignificant as myself could awaken an interest so marked in England. These papers were not the only parties surprised. I was myself not far behind them in surprise.*

Douglass was surprised by the kindness of the British people. They expressed outrage that he was a fugitive in America and raised enough money to buy his freedom. In 1845, his English friends presented Hugh Auld with $711.66, payment for the life of his slave. Frederick Douglass was now a free man.

Douglass no longer feared returning home. In 1847, after 20 months overseas, he returned to the United States. A crowd had gathered to welcome him, but Douglass pushed through them to catch a train to Lynn, Massachusetts. He couldn't wait to see his wife and children. Douglass missed much of their lives while he was in England, but his time there would affect him the rest of his life.

The people of England, who purchased Douglass's freedom, also supported his desire to start a newspaper. Douglass wanted white people to realize that blacks were not inferior. Showing that a black man could successfully maintain his own abolitionist newspaper would be a good start. His success also would be a beacon of hope to other black people. To aid in his cause, the British collected enough money for Douglass to buy a printing press.

Douglass set up his newspaper, *The North Star*, in Rochester, New York. The paper not only supported the antislavery cause, it also advanced the cause of equal rights for women. Rolling off the press for the first time on December 3, 1847, *The North Star* became a smashing success. Subscriptions increased rapidly in the United States, and copies of the paper were sold in Canada, Great Britain, Australia, and Mexico.

By February 1848, the newspaper was well established, and Douglass felt settled in Rochester. He traveled back to Massachusetts and packed up his family for the move. He wanted his family there to share in his success and good fortune. That year brought another blessing—the birth of their fifth child, a daughter named Annie.

That year, Douglass met abolitionist John Brown, a man of action rather than words. Brown helped slaves escape to Canada and aided an organization that protected slaves from slave catchers. He also joined the conflict over whether Kansas would be admitted to the Union as a free state or a slave state.

A copy of Douglass's newspaper, The North Star, *dated June 2, 1848*

For many years, the people of the United States continued to argue over the issue of slavery. Would new states be allowed to have slaves? Should slavery be abolished completely? By 1857, abolitionists like John Brown were making plans to do whatever it

Douglass delivered one
of his most famous
speeches on July 5,
1852, in Rochester,
New York. He told the
nation to wake up and
realize that while white
people celebrated
Independence Day on
July 4, millions of
blacks remained slaves.
"This Fourth of July is
yours, not mine. You
may rejoice, I must
mourn," he told the
crowd of about 600.
"What to the
American slave is your
Fourth of July? I
answer, a day that
reveals to him, more
than all other days in
the year, the gross injus-
tice and cruelty to
which he is the con-
stant victim."

might take to do away with slavery. Brown collected weapons
and enlisted men for an invasion
of the South. He planned to
raid an arsenal at Harpers
Ferry, where the Potomac and
Shenandoah rivers meet, and give
weapons to slaves. Once slaves
were armed, he expected they
would rebel against their captors.

At first, Douglass supported
Brown's plan. But he soon realized Brown's plan wasn't well
thought out. Douglass was con-
vinced his friend was walking
into a death trap at Harpers Ferry
and tried to talk him out of it.

Brown couldn't be stopped.
On October 16, 1859, with the
help of 21 men, Brown captured
the arsenal, but his success was
short-lived. The next day, Colonel
Robert E. Lee captured Brown
and his men. Brown stood trial
and was convicted of treason. On December 2, 1859,
he was hanged.

Even though he didn't actively participate in the
Harpers Ferry incident, Douglass became tied to it.

On that fateful day, Brown carried with him a note from Douglass, dated back to 1857, inviting him to dinner. Newspapers across the country printed the invitation. Virginia Governor Henry Wise called for the arrest of all Brown's allies, including Douglass. With the threat of capture looming, Douglass fled first to Canada and then to England. There he received the tragic news that his 11-year-old daughter Annie had died. Though fearful of being captured, Douglass returned home. In the meantime, Congress moved to close the whole Harpers Ferry affair, releasing Douglass from any involvement.

John Brown was hiding in the engine house at Harpers Ferry when Colonel Robert E. Lee stormed it on October 17, 1859.

John Brown's attack on Harpers Ferry had a lasting effect. The division over slavery grew deeper. Soon the country would be engulfed in the Civil War. ✒

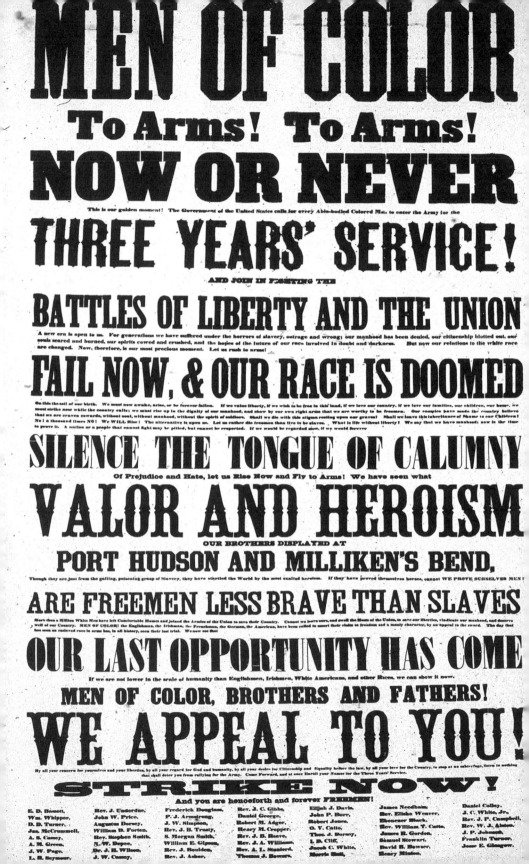

8 FIGHTING FOR THE UNION CAUSE

Chapter

ⲉᴑⲭⲟⲥ

Frederick Douglass soon became more involved in politics. With the presidential election of 1860 just around the corner, his choice was clear. He would support Illinois Republican Abraham Lincoln. Lincoln's name triggered anger in the hearts of Southern plantation owners who feared he would put an end to slavery. However, the name Lincoln filled Douglass's heart with hope.

Southern states threatened to leave the Union if Lincoln was elected president. Lincoln was indeed elected, and South Carolina became the first state to secede from the Union in December 1860. Another five states followed suit in January 1861. In all, 11 Southern states left the Union and started their own country—the Confederate States of America.

Posters were displayed to recruit black soldiers for the Union army during the Civil War.

> *Around 180,000 black soldiers fought in the Union Army during the Civil War. Most were slaves from the South who had fled to the North. Regiments made up entirely of black soldiers numbered 166, but most had white commanders. Only about 100 blacks were named officers during the Civil War.*

Lincoln refused to let the Union be dissolved, but he didn't want to go to war. However, on April 12, 1861, when Southern Confederates fired on the U.S. military post at Fort Sumter, North Carolina, the Civil War began.

Like many other abolitionists, Douglass was sometimes critical of the president's policies during the war and publicly voiced his opinions. One action that led him to speak out involved Lincoln's treatment of General John C. Frémont.

Early in the war, Frémont served as commander of the Union Army's Western Department. On his own, Frémont decided to take over the property of Missouri slave owners who were rebelling against the Union. He also freed all their slaves. While Douglass applauded Frémont for this, Lincoln responded to Frémont's unauthorized actions by removing him from command.

Douglass waited impatiently during the violent war for the president to announce freedom for slaves. Finally, on January 1, 1863, Lincoln read the Emancipation Proclamation, which freed all slaves in the rebelling states. To Douglass, this was a starting point for the rights of black Americans. He declared January 1, 1863, as their Independence Day.

Not long after the Emancipation Proclamation was announced, Massachusetts Governor John A. Andrew put out a call for volunteers. His request led to the formation of a unit of black soldiers—the 54th Massachusetts Volunteers. Douglass supported the Union cause by encouraging black people to volunteer for military service in the Union army.

In early 1863, Douglass began traveling around the North, enlisting black soldiers to fight for the Union. In his newspaper, now called *Douglass' Monthly*, Douglass placed an article asking for black volunteers. He couldn't have been prouder when the first recruit to sign up was his son Charles. His son Lewis also heeded his father's call to arms.

Charles Douglass, son of Frederick and Anna Douglass, was the first to volunteer for the all black unit, the 54th Massachusetts Volunteers.

Volunteering for military service was dangerous for blacks. Not only did black soldiers face the normal perils of war, but they were in danger of becoming slaves again if captured during battles in the South. To make matters worse, the Confederates passed a law in May 1863 stating that any black man captured in the fighting would be subject to the laws of the state where he was caught. Captured black soldiers would be punished like runaway slaves. In the South, the punishment was death.

Douglass was outraged. He said he wouldn't recruit more black soldiers if the rules of war were different for them than for white soldiers. He wasn't alone in his anger. "I cannot see the justice of permitting one treatment for them, and another for the white soldiers," Union General Ulysses S. Grant said.

Many people began criticizing the law and supporting the cause of black soldiers. The unfair law created sympathy for blacks among those who had not taken a stand on the slavery issue before.

Lincoln didn't ignore the new Confederate law and soon took action. In July 1863, he signed an order stating that for every Union soldier killed in violation of the laws of war, a rebel soldier's life also would be taken.

On August 10, 1863, Douglass met with Lincoln for the first time. He gave the president his full faith and support and personally thanked him for taking action on the matter. That same day, President Lincoln signed a letter written by the Department of the Interior making Douglass's freedom official and granting him all the rights of a free man.

Toward the end of the Civil War, Douglass began another speaking tour. This time, he asked not only that slavery be abolished, but he also asked for guarantees that blacks would be treated equally. That would be his next challenge. ✑

A letter dated August 10, 1863 officially granted Frederick Douglass the rights of a free man. Abraham Lincoln was one of the signers (sideways at bottom left).

9 LIFE AFTER THE WAR

༄

The Civil War ended in 1865. That year, on April 14, President Lincoln was assassinated by John Wilkes Booth at Ford's Theatre in Washington, D.C. Frederick Douglass became more determined to work for fairness for freed slaves, urging justice, not pity, for blacks.

The 13th Amendment to the U.S. Constitution, approved on December 6, 1865, abolished slavery. When the 14th and 15th Amendments were passed, the country moved toward more equality for citizens. But Douglass found they didn't make all things right for black Americans. The 15th Amendment gave black men the right to vote, but that didn't stop many Southern states from finding ways to keep them from casting their ballots.

Frederick Douglass in 1879 at the age of 61

Though equality may not have happened as quickly as Douglass wanted, strides were made during his lifetime. His son Charles saw the first elected black senator—Hiram Revels of Mississippi—sworn in during a session of Congress. Charles sat in the gallery during the historic 1870 ceremony. Later, he wrote to his father that he wished it were Frederick Douglass that had been sworn in that day.

After a fire mysteriously destroyed their home in Rochester in 1872, the Douglasses moved to Washington, D.C. Two years before the move, he had purchased the *New Era*, a Washington, D.C., weekly newspaper. Renaming it the *New National Era*, he used it as a place to further his agenda of equality. Unfortunately, in 1874 the venture folded. He had been able to obtain only a few white subscribers, the audience he really sought to educate on the issue of equality.

Douglass worked on several presidential campaigns, including the one that made former Civil War General Ulysses S. Grant the 18th president of the United States in 1868. He also helped in the campaign that got Grant reelected in 1872. Douglass's work for political causes was rewarded by a variety of government appointments. President Rutherford B. Hayes, the 19th U.S. president, named him U.S. marshal of the District of Columbia. A U.S. marshal had the authority to see that federal laws were carried out. This appointment had to be approved by the

U.S. Senate before becoming official. The Senate's approval was historic. It marked the first time the Senate approved the appointment of a black man to any position.

In 1882, Douglass suffered a great loss. His wife of 44 years, Anna Murray Douglass, suffered a stroke in July that left her paralyzed on her left side. Her death on August 4, 1882, left her husband devastated and depressed.

Frederick Douglass married Helen Pitts after his first wife died.

However, Douglass didn't remain alone. In January 1884, he married his former secretary Helen Pitts. The marriage caused quite a scandal because Helen was white. Not only did Douglass's children disapprove, but many members of Helen's family were angry. Gideon Pitts, Helen's father, was an abolitionist and a friend of Douglass, but when Douglass and Helen married, Gideon no longer welcomed him into his home.

Despite the difficulties, the couple loved each other and enjoyed their life together. In 1886 and

1887, they traveled to several countries, including Ireland, Italy, France, Greece, and Egypt.

In October 1889, they set sail again. This time they traveled to Haiti, where Douglass served two years as the U.S. minister, or representative, to the country. He resigned due to a disagreement with a U.S. policy to use the Haitian port town of Môle St. Nicholas as a navy refueling station. The couple returned to

Frederick Douglass, U.S. minister, at his desk in Haiti

Washington, D.C., in July 1891, where Douglass continued his work for civil rights, attending meetings and speaking on equality for blacks and women. On February 20, 1895, after attending a rally for women's rights, he came home to share an evening meal with Helen and tell her about his day. As he stood to mimic one of the speakers, Douglass fell to the floor and died of a heart attack.

Telegrams expressing sorrow came to the Douglass family from foreign dignitaries and U.S. congressmen. In Washington, D.C., black schools closed to mourn his death. After funeral services were held in Washington, D.C., Douglass's family accompanied his body to Rochester, New York, the place he had started *The North Star* and aided the Underground Railroad. There Douglass was laid to rest in Mount Hope Cemetery next to his first wife Anna and their daughter Annie.

Unlike his mother's grave, Douglass's final resting place was marked. The headstone was simple, but it bore the name of a free man—Frederick Douglass. ❧

> *Douglass's last home in Washington, D.C., was turned into a national historic site. Douglass's house, called Cedar Hill, welcomed many important visitors during his lifetime, including Susan B. Anthony, a leader in the woman suffrage movement, and abolitionist Harriet Tubman. Today, Cedar Hill stands as part of the National Park Service.*

DOUGLASS'S LIFE

1818

Born Frederick
Augustus Washington
Bailey in Tuckahoe,
Maryland, in February

1826

Sent to Baltimore,
Maryland, to live with
the Hugh Auld family

1833

Sent to St. Michaels,
Maryland, to live with
his new owner
Thomas Auld

1825

1821

Central American
countries gain
independence
from Spain

1826

The first photo-
graph is taken by
Joseph Niépce, a
French physicist

1833

Great Britain
abolishes slavery

WORLD EVENTS

1834

Rented out to farmer Edward Covey, known as a "slave breaker"

1836

Makes an escape plan but is discovered, jailed, and then released; returns to Hugh Auld in Baltimore; hired out as an apprentice in the shipyard

1838

Borrows papers from a free black sailor and escapes to New York; marries Anna Murray on September 15; changes name to Douglass and settles in New Bedford, Massachusetts

1835

1836

Texans defeat Mexican troops at San Jacinto after a deadly battle at the Alamo

DOUGLASS'S LIFE

1841

Hired as a speaker for the Massachusetts Anti-Slavery Society and begins touring the country

1839

Reads about the abolitionist movement in William Lloyd Garrison's newspaper *The Liberator*

1845

Publishes first autobiography, *Narrative of the Life of Frederick Douglass, an American Slave*; tours Great Britain, speaking about slavery; British friends purchase his freedom

1840

1840

Auguste Rodin, famous sculptor of *The Thinker* is born

1846

Irish potato famine reaches its worst

WORLD EVENTS

1863

Recruits black soldiers for the 54th Massachusetts Volunteers, the first regiment of black soldiers in the Civil War; meets with President Abraham Lincoln

1847

Returns to the United States a free man; buys printing press and publishes weekly newspaper, *The North Star*

1868

Campaigns for Civil War General Ulysses S. Grant for president

1865

1848

The Communist Manifesto by German writer Karl Marx is widely distributed

1858

English scientist Charles Darwin presents his theory of evolution

DOUGLASS'S LIFE

1882

Douglass's wife Anna dies August 4 after suffering a stroke

1884

Marries Helen Pitts January 24

1870

Takes over as editor of the *New National Era* in Washington, D.C.

1870

1869

The periodic table of elements is invented by Dimitri Mendeleyev

1877

German inventor Nikolaus A. Otto works on what will become the internal combustion engine for automobiles

WORLD EVENTS

1889

Appointed U.S. minister to the Republic of Haiti

1895

Dies February 20 in Washington, D.C.; is buried in Rochester, New York

1891

Resigns as minister to Haiti after disagreement with a U.S. policy

1890

1893

Women gain voting privileges in New Zealand, the first country to take such a step

DATE OF BIRTH: February 1818

BIRTHPLACE: Tuckahoe, Maryland

FATHER: Unknown, but Douglass
believed his father was white

MOTHER: Harriet Bailey

EDUCATION: no formal education

SPOUSE: Anna Murray Douglass
(1813-1882)
Helen Pitts (1837-1903)

DATE OF MARRIAGE: Anna Murray, September
15, 1838
Helen Pitts, January 24,
1884

CHILDREN: Rosetta (1839-1906)
Lewis (1840-1908)
Frederick Jr. (1842-1892)
Charles (1844-1920)
Annie (1849-1860)

DATE OF DEATH: February 20, 1895

PLACE OF BURIAL: Rochester, New York

IN THE LIBRARY

Douglass, Frederick. *Escape from Slavery: The Boyhood of Frederick Douglass in His Own Words.* New York: Knopf, 1994.

Douglass, Frederick. *Narrative of the Life of Frederick Douglass, an American Slave.* Boston: Bedford Books of St. Martin's Press, 1993.

Foner, Philip S., ed. *Frederick Douglass: Selected Speeches and Writings.* Chicago: Lawrence Hill Books, 1999.

Marten, James. *The Children's Civil War.* Chapel Hill, N.C.: University of North Carolina Press, 1998.

McFeely, William S. *Frederick Douglass.* New York: W. W. Norton & Company, Inc., 1991.

McIntire, Suzanne. *American Heritage Book of Great American Speeches for Young People.* New York: Wiley, 2001.

Streissguth, Thomas. *Slavery.* San Diego: Greenhaven Press, 2001.

Yancey, Diane. *Frederick Douglass.* San Diego: Lucent Books, 2003.

ON THE WEB

For more information on *Frederick Douglass*, use FactHound to track down Web sites related to this book.

1. Go to *www.facthound.com*
2. Type in a search word related to this book or this book ID.0756508185
3. Click on the *Fetch It* button.

FactHound will find the best Web sites for you.

HISTORIC SITES

The Frederick Douglass
National Historic Site
1411 W Street, S.E.
Washington, D.C. 20020
202/426-5961
To visit Cedar Hill where Douglass lived from 1877 until his death in 1895.

The Boston African American National Historic Site
In the heart of Beacon Hill neighborhood
Boston, Massachusetts
To visit the memorial to the African-American Massachusetts 54th Regiment

abolitionists
people who worked to get rid of slavery

apprenticed
working for and learning from a skilled worker for a certain amount of time

caulk
to fill with a substance to prevent leaking; make watertight

Confederates
people living in the states that seceded from the United States during the Civil War

overseers
people who supervised slaves working in the fields

rebel
soldier of the Confederate Army during the Civil War

stroke
a sudden weakness caused by the breaking or blocking of a blood vessel in the brain

Union
the Northern states that fought against the Southern states in the Civil War

washhouse
a building used or equipped for washing clothes

Chapter 2

Page 18, line 5: Frederick Douglass. *Narrative of the Life of Frederick Douglass, an American Slave.* Boston: Bedford Books of St. Martin's Press, 1993, p. 40.

Page 19, line 6: Frederick Douglass. *My Bondage and My Freedom.* Chicago: Johnson Publishing Co., Inc., 1970, p. 79.

Page 22, line 7: Ibid., p. 36.

Page 23, line 11: Ibid., pp. 36-37.

Chapter 3

Page 26, line 9: Ibid., p. 81.

Page 27, line 12: *Narrative of the Life of Frederick Douglass, an American Slave.* p. 54.

Page 29, line 1: Ibid., p. 52.

Chapter 4

Page 33, line 8: Ibid., p. 54.

Page 34, line 16: Ibid., p. 57.

Page 37, line 1: *My Bondage and My Freedom.* p. 113.

Page 38, line 17: *Narrative of the Life of Frederick Douglass, an American Slave.* p. 61.

Page 41, line 4: Ibid., p. 62.

Chapter 5

Page 46, line 4: Ibid., p. 71.

Page 49, line 21: Ibid., p. 72.

Page 50, line 22: Ibid., p. 74.

Page 52, line 19: *Narrative of the Life of Frederick Douglass, an American Slave.* p. 77.

Page 55, line 10: Ibid., p. 79.

Page 55, line 23: Ibid., p. 83.

Page 57, line 15: Ibid., p. 87.

Page 58, line 8: Ibid., p. 88.

Page 59, line 9: Ibid., p. 89.

Page 60, line 4: Ibid., p. 89.

Page 61, line 8: Ibid., p. 90.

Chapter 6

Page 64, line 1: Ibid., p. 91.

Page 65, line 10: Ibid., p. 92.

Page 65, line 23: Ibid., p. 92.

Page 68, line 3: *My Bondage and My Freedom.* p. 229.

Page 69, line 6: *Narrative of the Life of Frederick Douglass, an American Slave.* p. 98.

Chapter 7

Page 72, line 14: Ibid., p. 102.

Page 73, line 3: Ibid., p. 103.

Page 76, line 15: *My Bondage and My Freedom.* p. 282.

Page 79, line 4: Ibid., pp. 294-295.

Page 82, sidebar: *Narrative of the Life of Frederick Douglass, an American Slave.* pp. 142, 145.

Chapter 8

Page 88, line 8: William S. McFeely. *Frederick Douglass.* New York: Simon & Schuster, 1992, p. 227.

Select Bibliography

"Andrew Jackson." *The White House.*
http://www.whitehouse.gov/history/presidents/aj7.html

"Baltimore." *The Columbia Encyclopedia.*
http://www.bartleby.com/65/ba/BaltimorCit.html

Douglass, Frederick. *My Bondage and My Freedom.* Chicago: Johnson
Publishing Co., Inc., 1970.

Douglass, Frederick. *Narrative of the Life of Frederick Douglass, an
American Slave.* Boston: Bedford Books of St. Martin's Press, 1993.

"Frederick Douglass." *Africans in America.*
http://www.pbs.org/wgbh/aia/part4/4p1539.html

"Frederick Douglass." *The Frederick Douglass Museum & Cultural Center.*
http://www.ggw.org/freenet/f/fdm/

"Frederick Douglass." *The Frederick Douglass National Historic Site.*
http://www.nps.gov/frdo/freddoug.html

Library of Congress.

McFeely, William S. *Frederick Douglass.* New York: Simon & Schuster, 1992.

13th Amendment, 91
14th Amendment, 91
15th Amendment, 91
54th Massachusetts Volunteers, 87

abolitionists, 38-40, 41, 73, 76, 78, 80, 81-82, 86, 93, 95
Andrew, John A., 87
Anthony, Aaron, 9-10, 16, 43
Anthony, Andrew, 43-44
Anthony, Lucretia, 31, 33, 43, 44
Anthony, Susan B., 95
ash cakes, 26
Auld, Hugh, 31, 34, 61, 66, 79
Auld, Rowena Hamilton, 44
Auld, Sophia, 34-35, 36-37, 38, 65-66
Auld, Thomas, 31, 34, 37, 44, 52-53, 55, 61, 63

Bailey, Betsey (grandmother), 17, 18, 20, 23, 31
Bailey, Eliza (sister), 23
Bailey, Harriet (mother), 15, 17-18, 20
Bailey, Henry (slave), 56, 59
Bailey, Isaac (grandfather), 17
Bailey, Perry (brother), 23, 43-44
Bailey, Sarah (sister), 23
Baltimore, Maryland, 31, 34, 39, 61, 63, 66
Bondly, Beal, 29-30
Booth, John Wilkes, 91
Brown, John, 80, 81-82, 83

Cedar Hill house, 95
Chesapeake Bay, 51
Civil War, 13, 86-87, 87-88, 91
clothing, 18
Coffin, William C., 74
Collins, John A., 74-75
The Columbian Orator (book), 38
Confederate States of America, 85, 87-88
Covey, Edward, 46, 49-50, 51-52, 54-55
Demby (slave), 28-29

Department of the Interior, 88
Douglass, Anna Murray (wife), 66, 69, 72, 93, 95
Douglass, Annie (daughter), 80, 95
Douglass, Charles (son), 76, 87, 92
Douglass, Frederick
  alias of, 69, 71
  apprenticeship of, 63-65, 66
  arrest of, 57-61
  at Auld plantation (Baltimore), 34-35, 35-38, 44, 63
  at Auld plantation (St. Michaels), 44, 52
  beatings of, 11, 30-31, 44, 52-53, 54-55, 65
  birth of, 11, 15-16
  Cedar Hill house, 95
  childhood of, 9, 11, 18, 19-20, 22-23
  at Covey farm, 46-52, 54-55
  death of, 95
  Douglass' Monthly newspaper, 87
  education of, 11-12, 35-38
  escape attempts of, 53-54, 56-57, 58-59, 66-68
  freedom of, 79, 88
  at Freeland farm, 55-56
  at Great House Farm, 22-23, 25, 26, 27, 28, 31, 33, 43-44
  Harpers Ferry raid and, 82-83
  health of, 51-52
  lecture tour, 76-77
  marriages of, 69, 93
  at Massachusetts Anti-Slavery Society meeting, 74-75
  military recruitment by, 87, 88
  New National Era newspaper, 92
  The North Star newspaper, 13, 79-80, 95
  on oil ship, 73
  politics and, 85, 92
  siblings of, 23
  speaking tour, 75, 78-79, 82, 88-89
  surname of, 71
  as U.S. Marshal, 92-93
  world travel of, 94

Douglass, Frederick, Jr. (son), 76
Douglass, Helen Pitts (wife), 93
Douglass, Lewis (son), 73, 87
Douglass' Monthly newspaper, 87
Douglass, Rosetta (daughter), 73, 83

Emancipation Proclamation, 86

Fifteenth Amendment, 91
Fourteenth Amendment, 91
Freeland, William, 55, 57, 61
Frémont, John C., 86
fugitives, 12-13, 57, 68-69, 72, 74

Gardner, William, 63
Garrison, William Lloyd, 73, 74, 76
Gore, Austin, 28-29
Grant, Ulysses S., 88, 92
Great Britain, 78-79, 80
Great House Farm plantation, 20-23,
    25, 26-27, 28, 31, 33, 43-44

Hamilton (slave owner), 57, 61
Harpers Ferry raid, 82-83
Harris, Henry, 56, 59
Harris, John, 56, 58, 59
Hayes, Rutherford B., 92
Hester (aunt), 9-10, 13
household slaves, 28

Jackson, Andrew, 46
Jenkins, Sandy, 54, 56
Johnson, Mary, 71
Johnson, Nathan, 71

Lee, Robert E., 82
The Liberator newspaper, 73
Lincoln, Abraham, 85, 86, 88, 91
Lloyd, Daniel, 28
Lloyd, Edward, 15, 20, 26, 30
Lynn, Massachusetts, 76

Massachusetts Anti-Slavery Society,
    73-74, 76
Mount Hope Cemetery, 95

Murray, Anna. See Douglass, Anna
    Murray.

Nantucket Island, Massachusetts,
    73-74
*Narrative of the Life of Frederick
    Douglass, an American Slave*
    (Frederick Douglass), 78
New Bedford, Massachusetts, 69, 71,
    72
New National Era newspaper, 92
New York, New York, 68-69, 76
The North Star newspaper, 13, 79-
    80, 95

Old Barney (slave), 30
overseers, 21-22, 25, 28

Pitts, Gideon, 93
plantations, 11, 15, 20-22, 37
Price, Walter, 66

Revels, Hiram, 92
Roberts, Charles, 56, 59
Roberts, Ned, 9
Rochester, New York, 82
Ruggles, David, 69, 71

safe houses, 57
Sally Lloyd (ship), 33-34
secession, 85
slavery
    abolition of, 91
    beatings, 9-10, 11, 25, 27, 30-31, 44,
        52-53, 54-55, 65
    birthdays, 11, 16
    chores, 15, 25-26
    clothing, 18-19, 25-26
    debate over, 81, 83
    education and, 37
    escape from, 40-41
    food, 18, 26, 27-28, 45
    fugitives, 12-13, 57, 68-69, 72, 74
    household slaves, 28
    murder and, 29

overseers, 21-22, 25, 28
passes, 56-57
slave breakers, 46
songs, 22
South Carolina, 85
St. Michaels, Maryland, 44, 52
Sudan, 16
suffrage movement, 95

Thirteenth Amendment, 91
Tubman, Harriet, 40, 95
Tuckahoe, Maryland, 11, 15, 17

Underground Railroad, 16, 40, 57,
    69, 95
Union Army, 86, 87

voting rights, 91

Washington, D.C., 91, 92, 95
Wise, Henry, 83

Young Barney (slave), 30

Brenda Haugen is the author and editor of many books, most of them for children. A graduate of the University of North Dakota in Grand Forks, Brenda lives in North Dakota with her family.

Image Credits